Goodnight, Sweet Dreams, I Love You:
An Illustration of Unconditional Love

(Even Tough Women Can Crack Like Eggs Sometimes, Book 3)

Diane Morasco

J Fox Ink ™ Publishing
Published by J Fox Ink ™
Diane Morasco Enterprises ™ LLC
USA

Jfoxinkpublishing.com
A Morasco Media™ Company
This book is an original publication of J Fox Ink™
Publishing.
Edited by Tanya R. Taylor
Cover design: TRT Studios™

Table of Contents

Dedication...5

In Memory of 6

Acknowledgments & Sincere Gratitude.....................7

Note from Diane Morasco....................................9

Smashing The Dream 10

Words of Tenderness from My Hero........................11

Our DNA...12

Inspirational Quotes 15-34

Epilogue...35

Other Books by Diane Morasco 36

Exclusive Bonus Content....................................39-47

Jacob Fox..48

About The Author...50

About The Publisher 55

The Art of Storytelling with Morasco & Taylor 57

Newly Released Bestseller!

"Eloquent. Beautiful. Soulful. A winner!"
- Parris Afton Bonds, Co-Founder of Romance Writers of America,
Bestselling author and Namesake of the Parris Award

Even TOUGH WOMEN
Can
CRACK
Like
Eggs
Sometimes

Diane Morasco

www.dianemorasco.com

Dedication

To that precious caramel, dimpled, curly girl from the Bronx, we did it kid. We did it! To that precious caramel, dimpled woman created in New York and established in New Jersey, we did it, cookie cake. We did it!

My trio of blessings - Gin, Hope and Zulie, and every pet I've ever had, thank you for being my shelter in the storm. I carry you with me in everything I do.

Tanya R. Taylor, my heart holds all the words; and my actions, I pray, illustrates them.

And, lastly, Stink, Stank, Stunk. You want a hit. Give me an hour, plus a pen and a pad.

In Memory of

My grandparents, Edward Otto Williamson and Bertha Vivian Hoffman Williamson. It all started with the two of you.

General and Cocoa - your paw prints are emblazoned on my spirit. Xoxoxo

Acknowledgments and Sincere Gratitude

To the Taylor Family for showing me what it is to have a family — O, Tanya, Sadies, and Christian.

Thank you to my kindred Bahamian sister in avocados, in comedy, in cupcakes disguised as muffins, in empowerment, in encouragement, in giggles, in fitness, in SNARK, in tears, and in understanding. And in baking. Girl, ya better hop to it.

Writing is a solitary journey; however, I am blessed to have incredible writing cookie cakes to travel with me on my expeditions – Tanya R. Taylor, Beth Prentice, and Summer Prescott. Oh! Let's not forget the Ninja! Mikey may feel left out. *Giggling*!

To the ladies who add a shot of *Writing Vitamin C* to my day – Kristen Martin, Author DNC, Burgess Taylor, Tamara Woods, Hildie McQueen, Stefanie London, and Kami Garcia.

Thank you to Cinda. What a gift to have found a kindred spirit who accepts, guides, listens, and understands. Thank you for being the one I feel safe enough with to share the embedded wounds of my soul, to finally release them and to watch me heal from the manacles that were seared into me.

As always, thank you to all those who tossed stones instead of giving hugs; who spouted poison instead of showering me with encouragement and to those who told me every chance they could how they wished I was never born…it was just what I needed to keep me from becoming like you.

And to the one who shattered me with, "I wish we've never met" may you find rest from your demons.

Note from Diane Morasco

I am over the moon and filled with gratitude to present, *Goodnight, Sweet Dreams, I Love You: An Illustration of Unconditional Love, (Even Tough Women Can Crack Like Eggs Sometimes, Book 3)*.

I absolutely love inspirational quotes. I am inspired by them and reflect on them. I was so moved by the response I was getting about my debut novel teaser quotes, I decided to compile my chapter quotes from *Even Tough Women Can Crack Like Eggs Sometimes* into one volume for you, my readers. I have also included exclusive bonus content for you to enjoy.

I have always enjoyed sending encouraging quotes to empower others — a dollop of radiance during life's storms or to further illuminate their day. It is my hope that you are stirred by the words I've written and warmed by the spark glowing inside of you.

Always,
DM

Smashing The Dream

I wanted more than I came from and I wanted that with Jacob. I wanted us to be this power couple and give back to others and enjoy our life. I wasn't one to believe in fairytales, but I certainly wanted to have a *happily-ever-after* with Jacob.

"You took my abhorrent ashes and created wondrous beauty."

Words of Tenderness from my Hero

"Babe, you don't always have to be the tough girl."
"You don't have to act so tough, babe."
"Babe, you don't have to be afraid and push me away."
"I love you, Diane. I so love you, babe."
"I love you, Diane Nicole…you don't have to be the tough girl."
"Babe, I love you. I so love you."
"I love you, Diane. You don't have to be a tough girl with me."

Yes! Yes, I do. I have to hide behind the façade of being a tough girl because I learned at a young age to never show anyone your weakness. I learned people will use your weaknesses to destroy you. I learned this growing up on Long Island from my mother's DNA. And my love for you is my weakness.

"I love you, Diane. Stop. Babe, you don't always have to be the tough girl."

Yep, I do. If I'm not a tough girl you will see my fears, my insecurities, my scars, my shame, my wounds, my ugliness, my worthlessness, and you will take your love away. Yes, you – the one I cherish the most will discover what a hideous monster I am. And when you discover how horrid I am, you will take your love and abandon me.

OUR DNA
By Diane Morasco

I believed the best was yet to come
I believed there wasn't anything we couldn't get through
I believed in you and me
For eternity
Until you put your hands on me.

I understood the abuse from your past
I came from one too.
I understood how your parents succumbed to addiction
Poppin' pills, liquorin' up…and shootin' up
As did you.

I came from a household of boozin' up
Still I wanted better
Thought you did too.
Still I didn't give in to the insidiousness of my DNA
But you did
And that was okay
'cause I loved you unconditionally
And I reached out my hand for you to hold onto.

And I believed you were more than the savages you came from
Until you choked me.
I gave you my heart
My mind
My body
My soul
I believed you when you said
You did too.

And I believed you when you said
I was the love of your life.
I believed you when you said
You wanted to make me your wife
Until you almost killed me.

I believed you when you said
You didn't mean to do it
When you said, it was a "blackout"
I wasn't sure just what I believed
'cause all I remember was shutting down
Praying this wasn't really happening.

I wanted so desperately for you to get well
All the while your drug addiction, violent outbursts and alcohol
dependence took center stage
And made my world a livin' hell
And I slipped further into the abyss
I cried
I prayed
I lashed out
I retreated
To a world I escaped to when I was a kid
Alone with my pets
Getting lost in the pages of a book
Or writing
As the tears froze
As my soul withered
And as my spirit started to perish.

I stood by you when the vultures known as your DNA
Circled and swooped in
They didn't like the way I responded to you putting your hands on
me
They didn't like how I called the cops and had you arrested

You didn't like it either
You blamed me for your outbursts
You said I was the reason for it.

The little girl inside was too shattered to cry
'cause the man she loved was strangling the little boy she loved
inside
The damaged little boy…you
I loved you unconditionally
Despite the fact I didn't understand the world you came from
A mother, a father sticking needles in their arms
A sister not worthy enough to raise her kids
A little sister taking her clothes off for dollars
And a man so broken
He let the best thing to ever enter his life go
'cause there was a sick, twisted comfort in the familiar
And he answered the call of the savages who share the same
DNA.

One: The Barrier Ruptures

> *"I survived the suffering of my childhood.*
> *I was a tough kid. I was a tough woman until my hero came along and cracked the façade I was tightly encased in."*

Two: When You Hurt Me, I Shattered into Pieces

"As a child, I skillfully learned how to plug my tear ducts, so no one would use my agony against me, that is until you came along and inflicted a much deeper heartache unleashing the floodgates."

Three: You Can't Do That to Me

"You knew the chaos I came from. I knew the chaos you came from. Still, you traumatized my world."

Four: Let's Take It Back to Jersey

"I infused your spirit with my love as you flourished in my sunshine. I believed you were the lamplight to cast the shadows away, as I bravely chased yours."

Five: Renegade Jay Blaze Melts the Glacier

"Because of my abuse, my self-esteem came from my body parts. With your love, I am able to glimpse a reflection of beauty and grace shimmering beneath the filth I was made to believe I was."

Six: Texas Comes to Jersey

"The essence of my being is not knowing the love I have for you, but feeling the love I hold for you, and feeling the love you gift to me. I will always be grateful to God for you."

Seven: Babe and Daddy Build a Life

"I want to fall asleep listening to the symphony of your heart beating, and wake every morning to the miraculous orchestration of you breathing."

Eight: Oh, What a Night! Mid-September Back in '13

"You gave me a reason to believe in the magic of being one. You asked. I answered:
'Til Death Do Us Part'."

Nine: Aftershock

"You discover who you are when the one you cherish, the one who holds your heart, squeezes it because either they don't know what love is or they are too infected to let the tender nutrients heal them. What truly annihilates your being is seeing the pleasure they get from it."

Ten: Soul Rupture

"How do you mend the broken pieces to a beautiful mosaic when your hero ruptures your soul?"

Eleven: Jersey City

"Your words fillet me. Your promises are empty. All I ask, daddy, is please don't utter any more empty words; let your actions illustrate what's inside your heart."

Twelve: A Dollop of Heaven on Earth - 64 Newkirk

"It doesn't matter what I may or may not do in this crazy world of ours 'cause it holds no meaning if you aren't there beside me."

Thirteen: Exiting My Beloved Garden State

"I was smashed open by the love fusing from him to me. When I looked at him, I was rendered breathless by his exquisiteness. I knew he would always be imprinted within my soul."

Fourteen: Even Tough Women Can Crack Like Eggs
Sometimes

> *"And then it finally happened. Daddy caused a crack that started the shattering to Babe's soul. And Babe would not be the same again. He severed an artery in her core."*

Fifteen: You Can't Unring a Bell

> *"You can't unring a bell. Your actions sealed our destiny. Time ticks on; however, it can never mend what you severed."*

Sixteen: Please, Daddy, Wake Me From this Nightmare

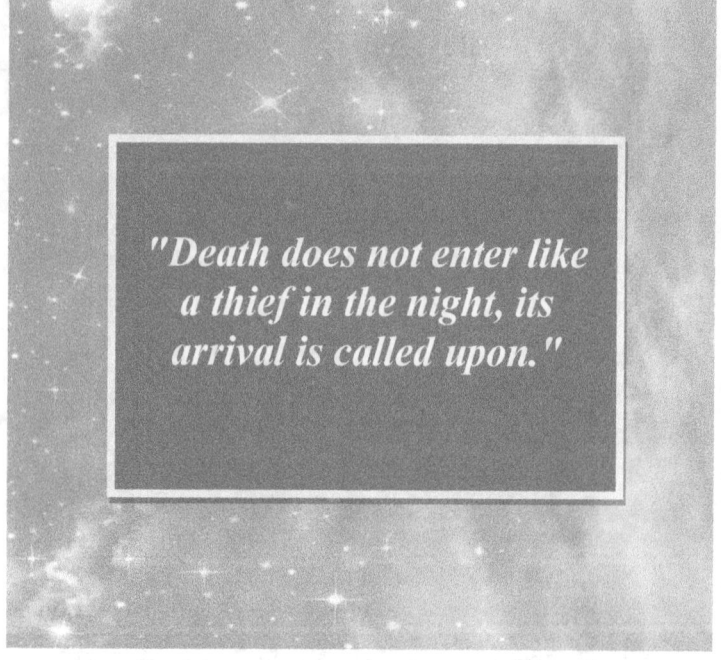

"Death does not enter like a thief in the night, its arrival is called upon."

Seventeen: Entering the Granite State

"The foundation of my childhood was built on sand. Menacingly, the ocean waves came crashing in. Decaying the powder, jarring my footing, as it collapsed, taking me along with it."

Eighteen: A Home for the Holidays before We Settle Down in Maine

"Mental illness wraps its claws around those afflicted and the loved ones around them."

Nineteen:
How it all Began for The Musician and The Writer

"The only way to achieve pure joy, absolute serenity, and unconditional love is to risk being stripped bare."

Twenty: Left in Ruin, I Crawl Through the Wreckage

"The excruciating pain you seared into me was something I did not expect from you. However, I must always keep in the forefront of my mind, I illuminate the sky, and you, you siphon my radiance with the chaos you create."

Epilogue

"It takes infinite strength to hide your own heartache. It takes omnipotent courage to show it."

"A man cannot respect a woman if he wasn't surrounded by women to respect."

OTHER BOOKS BY DIANE MORASCO

Even Tough Women Can Crack Like Eggs Sometimes (Book 1 in the Even Tough Women Can Crack Like Eggs Sometimes series)

Tough Wisdom to Transform Your Thoughts (Book 2 in the Even Tough Women Can Crack Like Eggs Sometimes series)

Inspirational Anchors to Ground You During the Waves of Life

Spirits Unleashed (An Old Sea Harbor Novel Novella)

COMING IN 2017

Remains to be Seen (An Old Sea Harbor Novel Young Adult Novel)

A Spark So Bright, Book 1 - The Casters (An Old Sea Harbor Young Adult novel)

The Curvalicious Girl's Guide to Life (Book 1 in The Curvalicious Girl's Guide to Life series)

My Trio of Blessings – How Gin, Hope and Zeus Saved a Wretch Like Me

Protecting Children in a Chaotic Environment (Book 4 in the *Even Tough Women Can Crack Like Eggs Sometimes series*)

Lessons from a Sly Fox (Book 5 in the *Even Tough Women Can Crack Like Eggs Sometimes series*)

Threshold – Diane Morasco and Tanya R. Taylor (Book 1 in *The Threshold Trilogy Collection of Short Stories*)

Snakes in the Garden: How My Faith, Intuition and Radiance Could Not Create The Legendary Salem Medium

UPCOMING OLD SEA HARBOR NOVELS

The Call of Death (An Old Sea Harbor Novel)

A Cast of Shadow. Book 2 - The Casters (An Old Sea Harbor Young Adult novel)

TOUGH SERIES IN PRODUCTION

Like Steel, I'm Not Easily Broken (Book 6 *Even Tough Women Can Crack Like Eggs Sometimes series*)

A Fractured Soul (Book 7 *Even Tough Women Can Crack Like Eggs Sometimes series*) – Dear God, I Suffered Miscarriages, am I Still a Mommy?

Tough Curves (Book 8 *Even Tough Women Can Crack Like Eggs Sometimes series*) – Eating Disorder and Body Image

I Can't is NOT in MY DNA (Book 9 *Even Tough Women Can Crack Like Eggs Sometimes series*)

www.dianemorasco.com

www.jfoxinkpublishing.com

EXCLUSIVE BONUS CONTENT

Grace beneath the Chaos

"You are the illumination to my darkness; the warmth to my essence; the oxygen to my lungs; the octane to my veins; the love I was blessed with after enduring so many years of chaos; the soothing balm that softens the roughness; the man that chases away the nightmares and paints a vibrant world of miracles, ecstasy, bliss, serenity, and paradise. I was frozen until you, Papa Turtle, melted the fortress with your renegade blaze."

Empty Shell

When all is said, and done
I'm nothing but an empty shell without you.
It doesn't matter what I may or may not do in this crazy world
of ours
'cause it holds no meaning
If you aren't there beside me.
Every breath I take is enhanced
Just by your existence
And I'm the first one to admit I wasn't expecting you.
You entered with all your beauty, bravery, and brashness
And changed the course of my direction
And led me straight to your exquisite heart.

You gave me a reason
You made me realize
My life had no real meaning until you.
I was stunned, frightened, and intrigued
And it was you who made me feel alive
It was you who made me recognize
I was just going through the motions without you.

I want to chase your demons away
With my love
I want to stand beside you
As you stumble
I want the universe and all its inhabitants to know
How honored I am to have you in my life.

I want to fall asleep listening to the symphony of your heart beating
And wake every morning to the miraculous orchestration of you breathing
'cause when all is said and done
My precious angel
I am nothing but an empty shell without you.

When I was trying to make sense of it all
When I was fighting what was happening
You illustrated sometimes there is no rhyme or reason.
When I didn't allow you to pull me into your chaos
You were always with me
As I retreated
And resurrected my fortress of emptiness
With every blade of agony embedded into my heart
With every ache seared into soul
With every tear shed
I realized more and more I was nothing
Nothing but an empty shell without you.

I want to chase your demons away
With my love
I want to stand beside you
As you stumble
I want the universe and all its inhabitants to know
How honored I am to have you in my life.
I want to fall asleep listening to the symphony of your heart beating
And wake every morning to the miraculous orchestration of you breathing
'cause when all is said and done
My precious angel
I am nothing but an empty shell without you.

Long Ago

Long ago there was an unwanted girl
Battered and neglected.
Long ago there was a broken boy
Confused and unaccepted.
The girl wanted desperately to be loved unconditionally
'cause that is how she loved
The boy just wanted to be understood
'cause no one gave a damn.

The girl vowed never to let anyone close enough to hurt her
'cause all she knew was agony.
The boy swore never to lose himself
And relinquish control
Until the night the two collided
When God's plan manifested.
Allied
Just as He intended
Destiny unfolded
Their hearts felt a trembling
Their souls felt a stirring
Lives changed that night
And their world was upended.
All along it was meant to be
Long ago Jacob and Diane were written in stone.

The girl shared her sadness and visions
The boy shared his fears and dreams.
Together

For always
They were linked
For always they are bonded.
The boy's love, humanity and strength brought the woman out
The girl's pureness, grace and devotion brought the man to the
surface
Together, they realized they were stronger as one United for
eternity.

Life in me

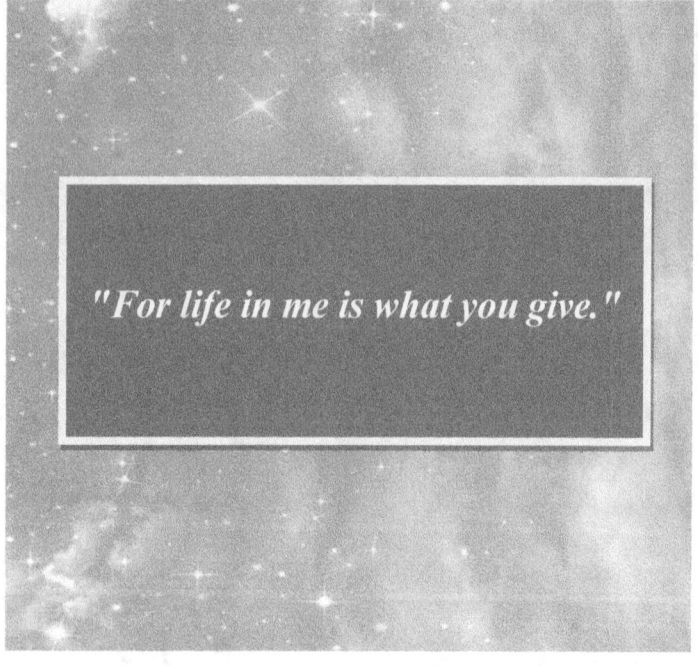

"For life in me is what you give."

Honored

> "I want the universe and all its inhabitants to know how honored I am to have you in my life."

An Ache Takes My Breath Away

"I love you with all of my being and I miss you with an ache that takes my breath away."

Obstacles

"There wouldn't have been any obstacles if there weren't any miracles destined for you."

Jacob Fox

If I'm about to take my last breath,
I want it to be whispering, "I love you, Jacob Fox and thank
you for the gift your presence has given me."
One, for feeling emotions I never imagined could flow from
me;
Two, for smashing the glass I was encased in to soar beyond
the iridescent stars and know it's because of you and your love
that I'm able to take flight;
Three, for life. You, Jacob Fox, are my everything, my reason,
every fantasy, hope, prayer, and wish. I hadn't a clue you were
what my heart wished for and didn't dare to dream.
Jacob Fox, you are the missing piece to my soul
You are the man who brings me light in the darkness
You are the lantern in my barren cave
You are the inferno who ignites my spark
You are my world.
Jacob Fox, you are my hero
The oxygen pulsating through my veins.
You are the sanctuary I seek amid life's torrential storms
You are the pinnacle of the mountains I climb
You are the man I adore, love, cherish, and treasure
Just as you are.
Life in me, Jacob Fox, is what you give
And without you there is no life.
I can't even say, I'm merely existing because that isn't
accurate;
Daddy, without you
I'm shutting down, retreating
Just breathing.

You bring out the best in me
And when you're acting out
You bring out the worse in me
And when I'm acting out
We both know it's an arsenal of attitude
It's a bozo and brat showdown
And we are both aware our childhood stuff sets off the
dysfunctional landmines.
And no one in this world, Fox, can claim to do what you do to
Morasco
For you are my kryptonite
You are the only one to get to me
To break me down
To lift me up
To tilt my universe on its axis
You, Jacob Fox, are my everything, my reason.
Jacob Fox, you are everything I wanted and never dared to
dream
Life in me, Jacob Fox, is what you give.

ABOUT THE AUTHOR

Diane Morasco is a triple fusion ethnically — vanilla, caramel and chocolate, and creatively — designer, media proprietor and writer. And now, she can add published author to the mix. Morasco was born in the Juicy Apple in the Bronx. She jokingly coined herself and smartly trademarked, Borough Babe™, after getting through the tough scenes in her debut novel, *Even Tough Women Can Crack Like Eggs Sometimes.* She did this by listening to hip-hop music from her youth and from time spent with her hero, reason and former fiancé - the namesake of her publishing company, J Fox Ink™.

She has publicly stated, "Apparently, the Bronx Girl and Jersey City Cookie Cake need this to get through these agonizing chapters. I am shaking my head 'cause the lil' Borough Babe™ inside likes to remind me of my formative years. Ya can take the chica outta the BX but obviously, the BX isn't having any of that Lawn Guy Land raised nonsense."

Morasco is the Founder, CEO, Chief Creative Officer, and Publisher of J Fox Ink™ (JFI); Founder, CEO, Chief Creative Officer of Diane Morasco Enterprises™ (DME), which is the parent company of Morasco Media™ (MM); The Book Resort™ (TBR), The Nicole Jerod Agency™ (TNJA), J Fox-Morasco Films™ (JFMF), The Glamour Vixens™ (TGV), and The Melting Plots™ (TMP).

She is the Co-Founder of The Art of Storytelling with Morasco and Taylor! ™, a mentorship program teaching aspiring writers The Art of Storytelling™.

Clearing the wreckage of her past, Morasco can finally concentrate on launching The Jacob Fox Collection™ by Diane Morasco, the clothing, jewelry and home décor line which was inspired by a man she once knew, who was "my reason for everything and who breathed life into me" before rebranding it as The Diane Morasco Collection™.

Morasco and International Bestselling Bahamian Author, Tanya R. Taylor, are cementing the Morasco and Taylor brand further by collaborating on a horror series. *Threshold,* the first spine-tingling trilogy collection of short stories in the vein of *The Twilight Zone,* will publish in 2017 with the next novel to follow in 2018 and the final one in 2019.

Morasco has also teamed up with Tayla Jade of Tayla Jade Photography™, a remarkable visionary from the Sunshine

Coast, Queensland. The two creative forces will be fusing their gifts with a line of inspirational décor and a series of coffee table books "to amplify the glow we all hold inside of us."

Morasco and Taylor are also collaborating with a USA Today Bestselling Author on a holiday themed mystery slated for late 2017.

Morasco has two more collaborative projects set for 2017, but is keeping it close to the vest as her schedule may have to push back the joint ventures until 2018.

Morasco is working behind the scenes taking her *Even Tough Women Can Crack Like Eggs Sometimes series* on the road with speaking engagements and workshops. Morasco plans on stepping out of her comfort zone with exclusive limited engagements later in 2017.

Morasco has film and television projects in development as well as a radio show to unveil in 2017, which is going to launch a sneak peek at the end of the year.

Spring 2014, she was asked to take over as co-author with a New England psychic with the J Fox Ink™ release, *Medium Rare*™.

September 2014, Ms. Morasco dropped the *Medium Rare*™

title to create, develop and license The Legendary Salem Medium™ brand for her client. She also became the author of the memoir she newly christened, *The Legendary Salem Medium: Memoir, Musings and Magic*. And in October 2014, Morasco temporarily relocated her family to a Salem, Massachusetts suburb to work exclusively with her client. In summer 2017, Morasco will release, *Snakes in the Garden: How My Faith, Intuition and Radiance Could Not Create The Legendary Salem Medium*. It deals with her experience with her former client. "I've been building my brand to provide an extraordinary sphere for my family with an intuitive spirit, a sharp eye and wise choices. Ultimately, it is my name on the company. I'm the Chief Cookie Cake. I'm not into parlor tricks, spectacle prophets or wickedness. I will not attach my name to anyone or anything that isn't nourishment for my soul."

Morasco first cut her teeth interviewing the immensely talented cast members of *Eureka*, *Warehouse 13*, and *Sons of Anarchy*, as well as Kurt Sutter himself, and countless writers, musicians, producers, and directors, celebrities – including the dashing Simon Cowell. She counts Ron Howard, Eddie McClintock and the *Sons of Anarchy* cast and team members for inspiring her to spread her wings into the film and television arena.

She is the former Editor-in-Chief for Alwayz Therro Magazine, former reviewer for RT Book Review and Long

Island Book Reviews, part of the now defunct Examiner. As her schedule permits, she guest scribbles for Blogcritics, which she credits for honing her skills.

Morasco has a genuine fervor for animals, butter cream cupcakes, *Supernatural*, *The Good Wife*, *Chicago Fire*, *Elementary*, *Castle*, *Major Crimes*, *General Hospital*, *Grimm*, the beach, cinnamon gum, music, movies, shooting pool, hiking, Italy, reading, and spa treatments!

Morasco likes to keep her professional life and her private life separate, but above all else, she can be found spending time with her trio of blessings – Gin, Hope and Zeus, creating and traveling the globe. And now that she has partnered with Tanya R. Taylor in The Bahamas and Tayla Jade in the land of Oz, globetrotting is par for the course. She just has to figure out how to travel with her trio of blessings when leaving the States.

ABOUT THE PUBLISHER

THEN

On May 29, 2013, Diane Morasco - Founder, CEO and Chief Creative Officer of Diane Morasco Enterprises LLC™ officially unveiled its Morasco Media™ publication division J Fox Ink™ in honor of her hero and reason, Jacob Fox.

With the inaugural 2014 launch of the J Fox Ink™ imprint, showcasing a diverse array of debut and previously published authors, J Fox Ink™ Publishing is the first amalgamated independent publisher and publishing house offering literary representation, media packaging and publishing.

In addition to the J Fox Ink™ imprint, Diane Morasco has added a young-adult imprint, Little Jake™ and a children's imprint, Lil' Fox™. She proudly articulates the Lil' Fox™ name was conceived during a brainstorming session with her hero, reason, fiancé and imprint namesake, Jacob Fox.

NOW

Founder, CEO, Chief Creative Officer, and Publisher Diane Morasco is ready to follow the guidance of ex-fiancé and imprint namesake to stop taking on clients and spearhead the company exclusively with her "phenomenal talent". As of November 2016, J Fox Ink™ will exclusively be Diane Morasco's Word Atelier.

THE ART OF STORYTELLING
WITH MORASCO AND TAYLOR™

It started with a whisper in The Granite State. It was this whisper that led Diane Morasco to take heed. Listening to the inner stirrings of her creative genius, she came up with an idea (she has a lot of those) and decided she wanted to give back to the community that rescued her from a chaotic childhood.

On June 30, 2016, she shared her vision with the prolific storytelling phenomenon,
Tanya R. Taylor. That day, The Art of Storytelling with Morasco and Taylor™ was created.

The Curvalicious Visionary™ and The Prolific Storytelling Phenomenon agreed to kick off 2017 by joining forces to teach aspiring writers The Art of Storytelling™.

International Bestselling author, Taylor, and Media Proprietor and Author, Morasco, know the importance of giving back and what better way is there than by helping other writers cross over the bridge from aspiring writers to published authors.

 Morasco and Taylor are Writers passing it on one word at a time! ™

GIVE A BOOK AND CREATE A MEMORY™

Please donate a book to your local women's shelter, hospital, library, nursing home, or school. Every book you donate will be a gift that will keep on giving long after the reader reaches "The End" and together we will Give a Book and Create a Memory™ – Diane Morasco

DON'T MISS EXCLUSIVE CONTENT
FROM DIANE MORASCO

Visit the author's website at:
www.dianemorasco.com

"Eloquent. Beautiful. Soulful. A winner!"

- Parris Afton Bonds, Co-Founder of Romance Writers of America,
Bestselling author and Namesake of the Parris Award

Even TOUGH WOMEN

Can

CRACK

Like

Eggs

Sometimes

Diane Morasco

www.dianemorasco.com

www.ingramcontent.com/pod-product-compliance
Lightning Source LLC
Chambersburg PA
CBHW060225290526
45789CB00003B/1418